100 CLASSICAL PIECES FOR ALTO SAX
GRADED

Published by
Hal Leonard

Exclusive Distributors:
Hal Leonard
7777 West Bluemound Road
Milwaukee, WI 53213
Email: info@halleonard.com

Hal Leonard Europe Limited
42 Wigmore Street
Marylebone, London, W1U 2RY
Email: info@halleonardeurope.com

Hal Leonard Australia Pty. Ltd.
4 Lentara Court
Cheltenham, Victoria, 3192 Australia
Email: info@halleonard.com.au

Order No. AM995588
ISBN 978-1-84772-751-4
This book © Copyright 2008 Hal Leonard

Edited by Jenni Wheeler.
Music processed by Camden Music.
Printed in the EU.

www.halleonard.com

GRADING NOTES

The pieces in this book have been carefully graded according to
various criteria such as rhythmic complexity, phrasing, tempo, key, range, etc.
Look for the number of stars for each piece to give you
an idea of the approximate playing level.
All musicians have particular strengths and weaknesses,
so the grading offered here should be taken as a suggestion only.

Generally, pieces with one star have simple rhythms,
straight forward phrasings and few difficult intervals;
essentially diatonic and in easier keys.

Pieces with two stars will have more challenging passages,
perhaps containing more rhythmic complexity,
more advanced key signatures and possibly explore a wider
range on the instrument.

Three-star pieces may include chromaticism,
challenging articulation and more advanced positioning.
Read through rhythms and keys before playing, and check for
time-signature changes and correct phrasing.

Air On The G String

Composed by Johann Sebastian Bach

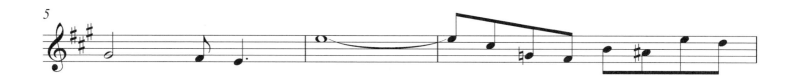

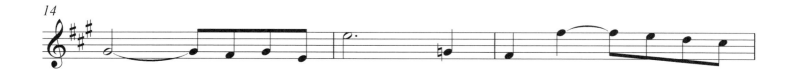

Allegretto
(from 'Symphony No.7', 2nd Movement)

Composed by Ludwig van Beethoven

Adagietto
(from 'Symphony No.5', 4th Movement)

Composed by Gustav Mahler

Anvil Chorus
(from 'Il Trovatore')

Composed by Giuseppe Verdi

Autumn
(from 'The Four Seasons')

Composed by Antonio Vivaldi

Allegro

Ave Maria

Composed by Charles Gounod

Ave Verum Corpus, K618

Composed by Wolfgang Amadeus Mozart

Barcarolle
(from 'The Tales Of Hoffmann')

Composed by Jacques Offenbach

Barcarolle tempo

16

The Blue Danube

Composed by Johann Strauss

Moderato con rubato

D.C. al Coda

✠ *Coda*

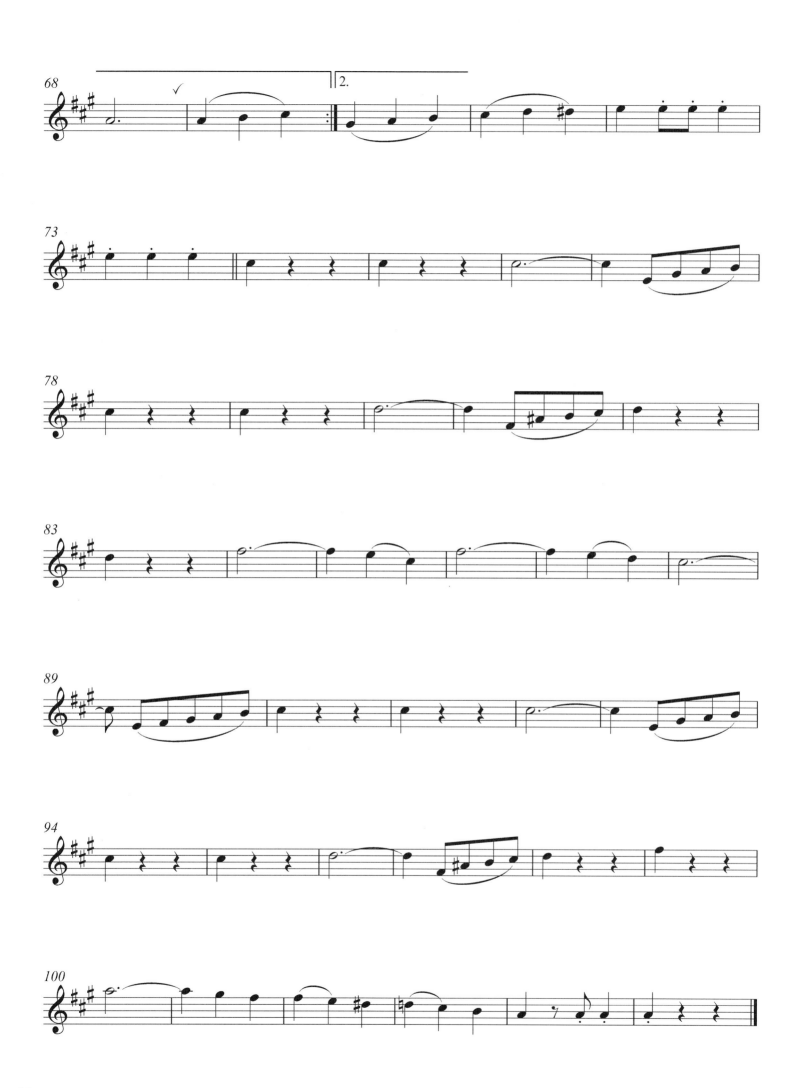

20

Bridal March

Composed by Richard Wagner

Brindisi
(from 'La Traviata')

Composed by Giuseppe Verdi

Capriccio Italienne

Composed by Peter Ilyich Tchaikovsky

The Can-Can

Composed by Jacques Offenbach

Canon in D

Composed by Johann Pachelbel

Lento

mp

poco rit.

mf

Poco andante

poco rit.

Più mosso

poco rit.

mf

Molto allegro

poco cresc.

poco rit.

Più mosso

molto rit.

Tempo I°

poco rit.

Caprice No.21

Composed by Niccolò Paganini

Chorale St. Anthony

Composed by Franz Joseph Haydn

Adagio

Celeste Aida
(from 'Aida')

Words by Antonio Ghislanzoni & Music by Giuseppe Verdi

D.C. al Coda   Coda

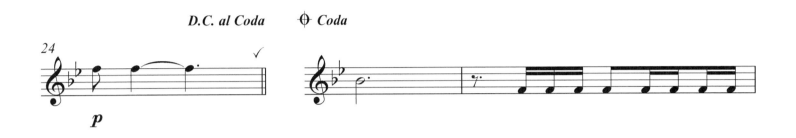

Clair De Lune

Composed by Claude Debussy

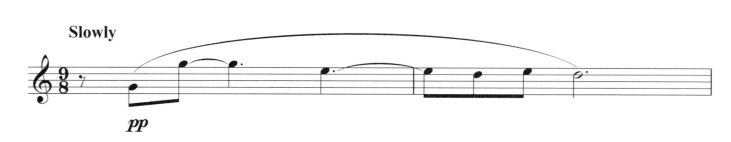

poco cresc.

poco dim.

dim. poco a poco

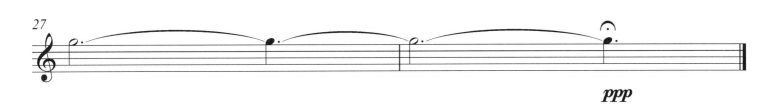

ppp

Dance Of The Blessed Spirits
(from 'Orfeo ed Euridice')

Composed by Christoph Willibald von Gluck

Andantino

Dance Of The Hours
(from 'La Gioconda')

Composed by Amilcare Ponchielli

Moderato

Danse Des Mirlitons

Composed by Peter Ilyich Tchaikovsky

36

Emperor Waltz

Composed by Johann Strauss

Tempo di valse

ben legato

Eine Kleine Nachtmusik, K525
(1st Movement: Allegro)

Composed by Wolfgang Amadeus Mozart

España

Composed by Emmanuel Claude Alexis Chabrier

Allegro con brio

Fantaisie Impromptu

Composed by Frédéric Chopin

Flower Duet
(from 'Lakmé')

Composed by Léo Delibes

Für Elise

Composed by Ludwig van Beethoven

Medium tempo

Gaudeamus Igitur

Composed by Johannes Brahms

Grand March
(from 'Aida')

Composed by Giuseppe Verdi

Habañera
(from 'Carmen')

Composed by Georges Bizet

The Happy Farmer

Composed by Robert Schumann

Allegro ma non troppo

Hallelujah Chorus
(from 'The Messiah')

Composed by George Frideric Handel

Moderato

rit.

ff

Hornpipe
(from 'Water Music')

Composed by George Frideric Handel

Allegro

rall.

51

Humoresque

Composed by Antonin Dvořák

Invitation To The Dance

Composed by Carl Maria Von Weber

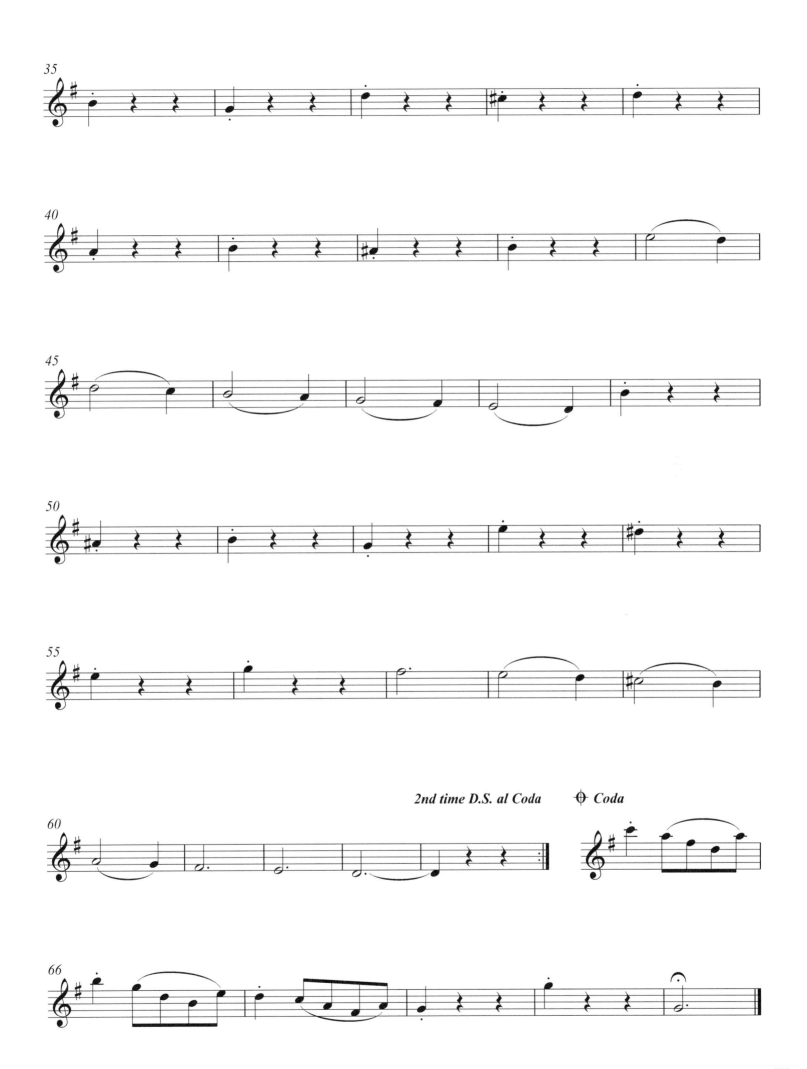

2nd time D.S. al Coda   Coda

The Harmonious Blacksmith

Composed by George Frideric Handel

Moderato

56

Jerusalem

Composed by Hubert Parry

Jesu, Joy Of Man's Desiring

Composed by Johann Sebastian Bach

58

Jupiter
(from 'The Planets Suite')

Composed by Gustav Holst

La Donna È Mobile
(from 'Rigoletto')

Words by Francesco Maria Piave & Music by Giuseppe Verdi

Land Of Hope And Glory
(Pomp And Circumstance March No.1)

Composed by Sir Edward Elgar

Allegro (largamente)

Largo
(from 'Xerxes')

Composed by George Frideric Handel

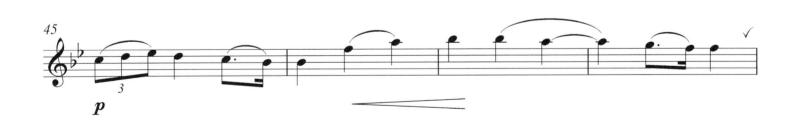

Largo
(from 'The New World Symphony')

Composed by Antonín Dvořák

Slowly

66

Lullaby

Composed by Johannes Brahms

Liebestraume: Notturno No.3 in A♭

Composed by Franz Liszt

March Of The Toys
(from 'The Nutcracker Suite')

Composed by Peter Ilyich Tchaikovsky

Tempo di marcia

70

March To The Scaffold
(from 'Symphonie Fantastique')

Composed by Hector Berlioz

Marche Militaire

Composed by Franz Schubert

(cue)

f

ff mp

f

f

(cue)

Fine

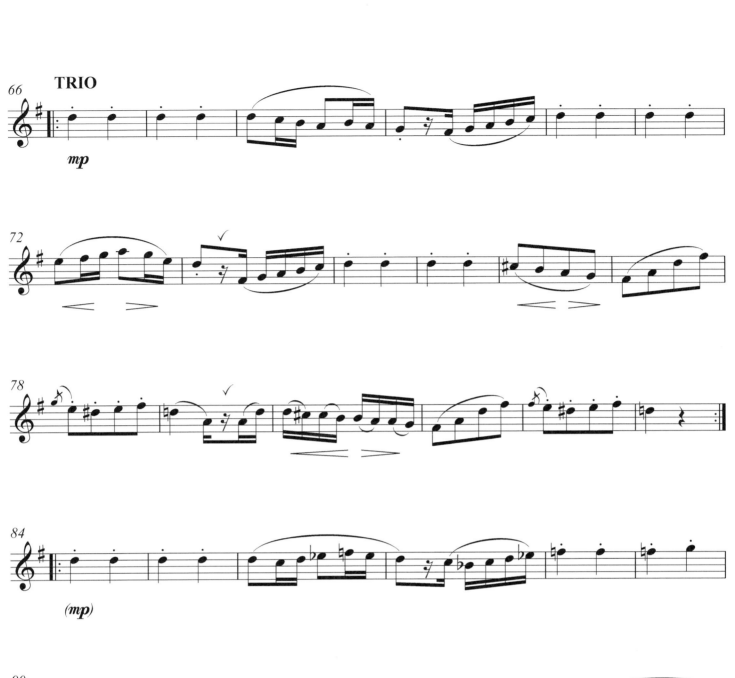

2nd time D.C. al Fine

Mazurka Op.7, No.1

Composed by Frédéric Chopin

Meditation
(from 'Thaïs')

Composed by Jules Massenet

Melody in F

Composed by Anton Rubinstein

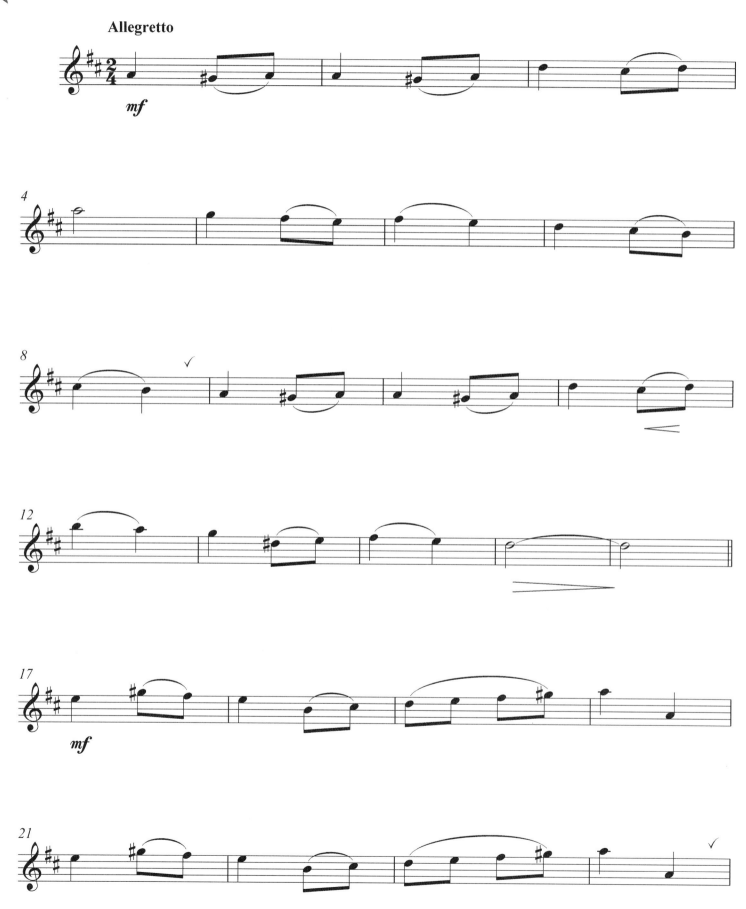

Minuet in G

Composed by Ludwig van Beethoven

D.C. al Fine

Minuet in G

Composed by Johann Sebastian Bach

Nocturne
(from 'A Midsummer Night's Dream')

Composed by Felix Mendelssohn

Minute Waltz

Composed by Frédéric Chopin

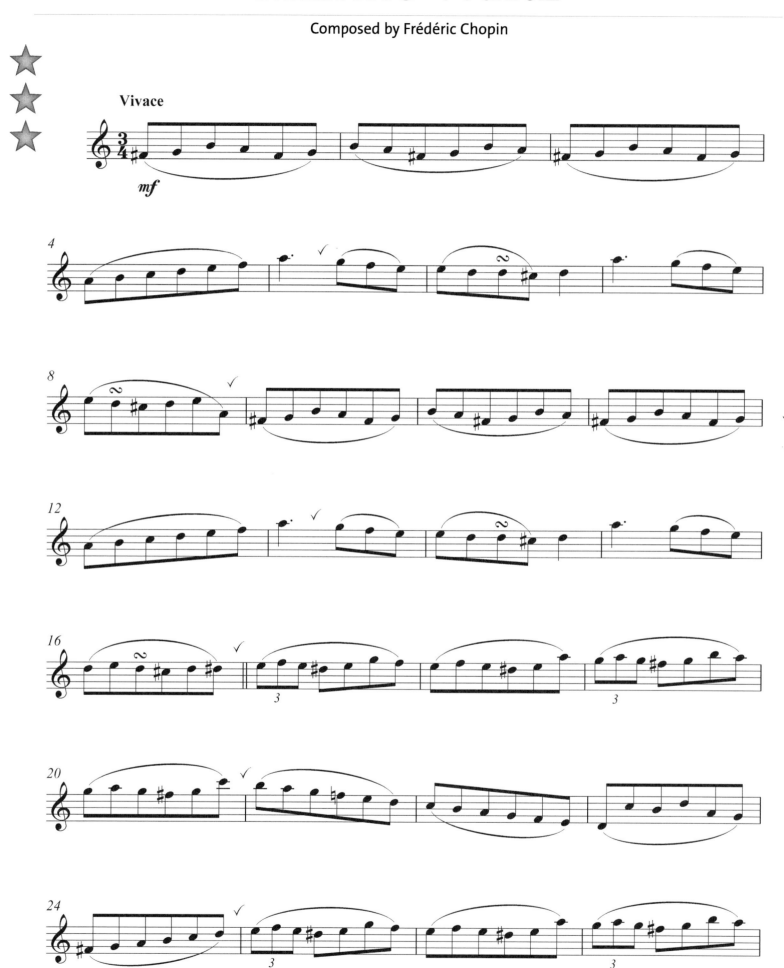

Morning
(from 'Peer Gynt')

Composed by Edvard Grieg

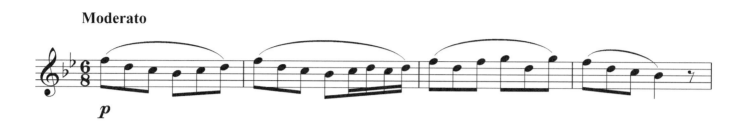

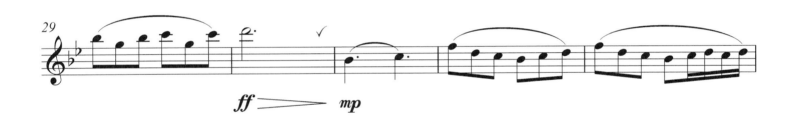

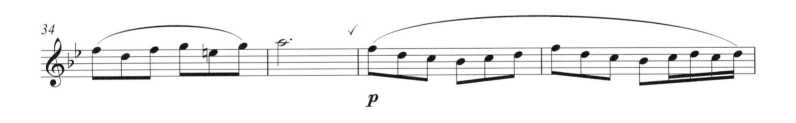

A Musical Joke

Composed by Wolfgang Amadeus Mozart

Nimrod
(from 'Enigma Variations')

Composed by Sir Edward Elgar

Adagio molto

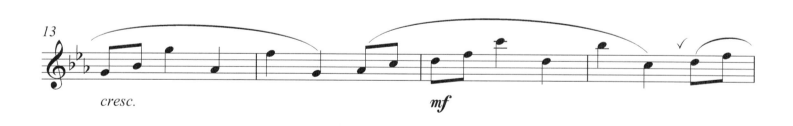

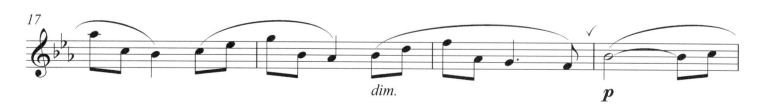

90

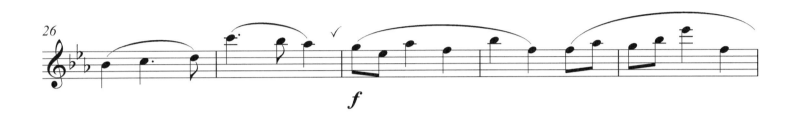

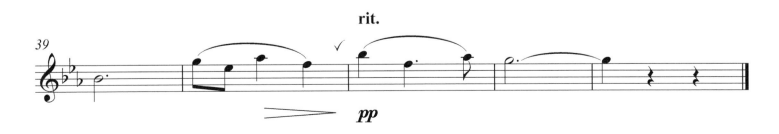

Norwegian Dance No.2, Op.35

Composed by Edvard Grieg

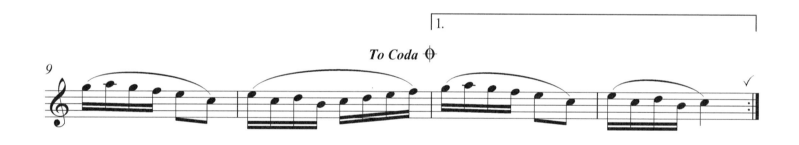

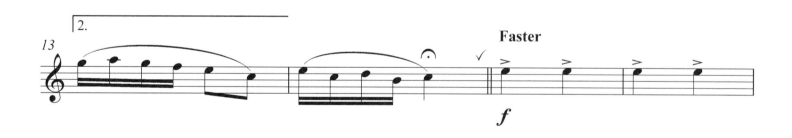

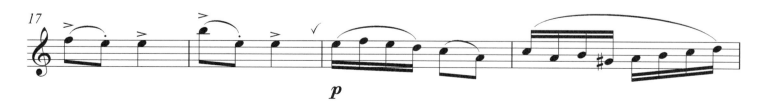

D.C. al Coda

Nocturne from String Quartet

Composed by Alexander Borodin

O For The Wings Of A Dove

Composed by Felix Mendelssohn

Ode To Joy
(from 'Symphony No.9', 4th Movement)

Composed by Ludwig van Beethoven

On Wings Of Song

Composed by Felix Mendelssohn

Theme from 'Pathétique Sonata'

Composed by Ludwig van Beethoven

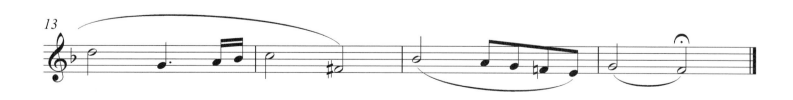

Piano Concerto No.1 in B♭ minor

Composed by Peter Ilyich Tchaikovsky

Molto grandioso

Piano Concerto No.21 in C major
(Theme from 'Elvira Madigan')

Composed by Wolfgang Amadeus Mozart

Pilgrims March
(from 'Tannhäuser')

Composed by Richard Wagner

Polonaise Op.53

Composed by Frédéric Chopin

Polovtsian Dance
(from 'Prince Igor')

Composed by Alexander Borodin & Completed by Nikolai Rimsky-Korsakov & Alexander Glazunov

Prelude Op.28, No.7

Composed by Frédéric Chopin

Promenade
(from 'Pictures At An Exhibition')

Composed by Modest Mussorgsky

Radetzky March, Op.228

Composed by Johann Strauss I

Marziale

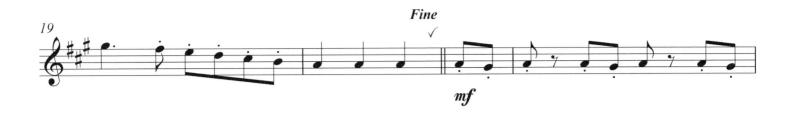

sempre stacc.

Rondo in D minor
(from 'Abdelazer')

Composed by Henry Purcell

Rosamunde Overture

Composed by Franz Schubert

Moderato
BALLET MUSIC

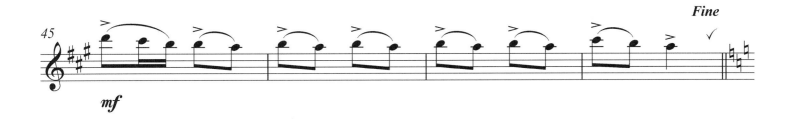

Romeo And Juliet

Composed by Peter Ilyich Tchaikovsky

Sarabande
(from the ballet 'Solitaire')

Composed by Malcolm Arnold

Sarabande
(from 'Suite XI')

Composed by George Frideric Handel

Lento

Spartacus
(Love Theme)

Composed by Aram Khachaturian

The Skater's Waltz

Composed by Emile Waldteufel

Spring
(from 'The Four Seasons')

Composed by Antonio Vivaldi

The Surprise Symphony

Composed by Franz Joseph Haydn

Allegretto

Spring Song

Composed by Felix Mendelssohn

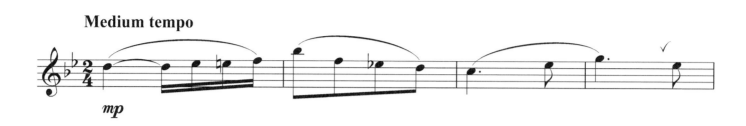

124

D.C. al Coda

Coda

Theme from Swan Lake

Composed by Peter Ilyich Tchaikovsky

Moderato

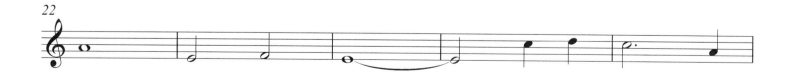

126

Symphony No.3 in F

Composed by Johannes Brahms

Theme from Symphony No.5, Op.67
(1st Movement)

Composed by Ludwig van Beethoven

Symphony No.40
(Theme)

Composed by Wolfgang Amadeus Mozart

Allegro molto

Symphony No.6 'Pastoral'
(5th Movement)

Composed by Ludwig van Beethoven

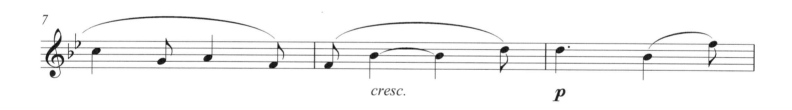

Tambourin

Composed by François Gossec

Tales From The Vienna Woods

Composed by Johann Strauss

To A Wild Rose

Composed by Edward MacDowell

cresc. poco a poco

f

p

mp

Toreador's Song
(from 'Carmen')

Composed by Georges Bizet

Träumerei

Composed by Robert Schumann

Trout Quintet

Composed by Franz Schubert

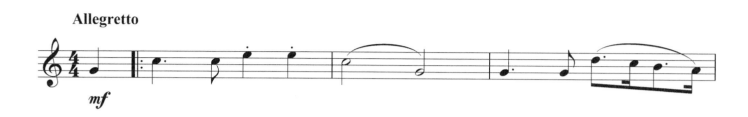

142

Violin Concerto
(2nd Movement)

Composed by Johannes Brahms

Trumpet Voluntary

Composed by Jeremiah Clarke

Marziale

Turkish March

Composed by Wolfgang Amadeus Mozart

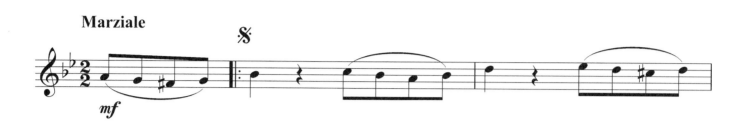

Waltz

Composed by Johannes Brahms

Waltz
(from 'Coppélia')

Composed by Léo Delibes

William Tell Overture
(Finale)

Composed by Gioacchino Rossini

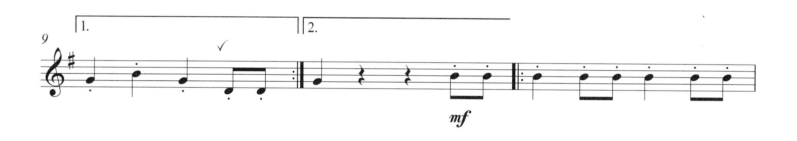

150

Waltz Of The Flowers
(from 'The Nutcracker Suite')

Composed by Peter Ilyich Tchaikovsky